T0129572

STARDUST TO STARDUST

Laughing at Life's Lapses

STARDUST TO STARDUST

Laughing at Life's Lapses

CLAUDINE K. SEIBERT

BALBOA.
PRESS

A DIVISION OF HAY HOUSE

This book is a work of non-fiction. Unless otherwise noted, the author
and the publisher make no explicit guarantees as to the accuracy of
the information contained in this book and in some cases, names of
people and places have been altered to protect their privacy.

Balboa Press books may be ordered through booksellers or by contacting:

Balboa Press
A Division of Hay House
1663 Liberty Drive
Bloomington, IN 47403
www.balboapress.com
1 (877) 407-4847

Because of the dynamic nature of the Internet, any web addresses or links contained in
this book may have changed since publication and may no longer be valid. The views
expressed in this work are solely those of the author and do not necessarily reflect the
views of the publisher, and the publisher hereby disclaims any responsibility for them.

The author of this book does not dispense medical advice or prescribe the use
of any technique as a form of treatment for physical, emotional, or medical
problems without the advice of a physician, either directly or indirectly. The
intent of the author is only to offer information of a general nature to help you
in your quest for emotional and spiritual well-being. In the event you use any
of the information in this book for yourself, which is your constitutional right,
the author and the publisher assume no responsibility for your actions.

Any people depicted in stock imagery provided by Getty Images are
models, and such images are being used for illustrative purposes only.
Certain stock imagery © Getty Images.

Print information available on the last page.

ISBN: 978-1-9822-2494-3 (sc)
ISBN: 978-1-9822-2495-0 (e)

Balboa Press rev. date: 04/03/2019

The best way to predict your future is to create it.

—Abraham Lincoln

Contents

Introduction

WHEN I TELL PEOPLE that I'm an only child they often get jealous or feel sorry for me. To my firstborn, middle-child, and lastborn friends, the subject of my first book, SCARS TO STARS: REFLECTIONS OF A DUBIOUS DAUGHTER, explains how I left my friends, a wonderful job, and a little bit of prime real estate in Manhattan in order to care for my ailing parents. I spent eighteen months at that life-changing task and it burnt me to a crisp. Heck, just relocating from New York City to Florida could fry anyone's brain, morale, and body. Yet, I managed to maintain a comic viewpoint. Along the way I provide what I believe are essential tips on how to survive and thrive when your world collapses around you.

My second venture, STARDUST TO STARDUST: LAUGHING AT LIFE'S LAPSES, is the product of the protective mental activity I developed to endure this roller coaster ride known as our time on Earth. Yes, it's occasionally necessary to spin on the ground in a fit of desperation and tears, but, eventually, we must scramble to our feet and get on with the rodeo. The alternative is not a pretty picture: Imagine being pulverized by life's disappointments and turning into gravel. Bumps in the road are important lessons since our lives are spent in a gigantic classroom to which we have been assigned, as Schopenhauer points out, simply by being born. (This observation also comes from your humble narrator, a writer in the middle stages of life, who has acquired her fair share of welts.)

If you're anything like me, you probably daydream now and then of knocking off your professors and peers or simply waving a white flag of surrender. Well, guess what? As any Buddhist, Christian, or self-respecting existentialist can tell you, the game isn't about that kind of overreaction. I envision life as a continual replay of Robert Crumb's famous comic, "Keep on Truckin'."

Fortunately, I continue to breathe and am eager to share my latest quirky views on everything from coffee to airports. Generating grins galore is one of the primary defense mechanisms I've nurtured. Think of how many times you've heard someone yelp, "You have to laugh or you'll cry" … that sums up how you'll spend your time with the following chapters.

I'm in the habit of sharing quotations that may assist people's evolution. My latest find is from Marianne Williamson's eternal calendar, A Year of Daily Wisdom. I'm currently attempting to better myself by practicing what she preaches, "Changes in life are always going to happen; they're part of the human experience. What we can change, however, is how we perceive them. And that shift in our perception is a miracle."

I often jest that I'm pregnant with myself. That's the only possibility for me. I'm too selfish to carry anything within my body except for an occasional idea or a catchy phrase. So, fasten your seat belt and cheer me on as I exercise my right to express opinions. I'll propel you into a world where we can face the absurdities of existence together with a smile upon your face.

I'd like to toast Michael Christian and Diane Bryson for being supportive and generous editors.

Super Florida

FLORIDA IS A LAND of superlatives. Even if you are a bona fide world traveler, you'll have to admit that there are outstandingly beautiful skies here. The islands of the Caribbean, Mediterranean countries, and Scotland's Isle of Skye have a run for their money. It doesn't matter if it's a sunny or overcast day. The range of colors and variety of three-dimensional clouds provide an emotional impact which can turn just about anyone into a stupefied drooler. I've oohed and aahed for miles when simply running errands.

As for many of the drivers in The Gulf State, that's when you can apply the label of super stupid. People hardly ever use their blinkers which can be downright deadly in a place where U-turns are legal on almost every block. I recommend upping your life and car insurance premiums if you plan to shop at Walmart. Visit your local priest or rabbi if you intend to visit a Super Walmart. The parking lot is like playing a reality version of Frogger. You'll be wearing skulls and crossbones before you hobble to the entrance.

An unofficial term for the northwestern sector of Florida is The Panhandle. The whole state should be nicknamed The Frying Pan. Leathery skin has a new and deeper meaning here. Some people look super old in their forties and fifties. The more aged sun worshippers look like walking fossils.

I'm at a stage in life when I actually care how much sun penetrates my skin especially since I live in The Alligator State. In order to avoid a reptilian visage, I decided to get my car windows tinted. I began observing different vehicles, shopping around, and asking questions. I knew right away that I didn't want the do-it-yourself tinting because that method resulted in what appeared to be a bubbling virus. I'm sure vision is highly obscured because of the curdling black welts all over the glass. It must be like trying to see out of an active volcano.

I also noticed that innumerable cars, vans, and SUVs looked like pimp mobiles because their windows were so black that they were opaque. I often wondered what those people were doing hiding behind plastic veils of darkness. I was told this particular type of super tinting was against the law which caused guilty drivers to be fined repeatedly by police. Fortunately, I was given the choice between legal or illegal tinting. How long did I have to think about that decision for God's sake? Now, my car is much cooler and I haven't aged a decade in the last few months but I can't see a thing especially at night and when I'm in reverse. Life's a trade-off, right?

The Everglade State has more than its fair share of tourists, surfers, beach bunnies, millionaires, and paupers. It also lays claim to super old automobiles and people. I swear that some of the vehicles are nothing more than two axles and some seats. You'll often see cars that appear to be driving themselves because the operator can barely see over the dashboard. You ask yourself, "Is there a child or a centenarian behind the wheel?" Both individuals would produce the same erratic behavior from the car. I hope when I'm ancient that someone has mercy on me and drives my carcass around in a car with tinted windows. Ripley's Believe it or Not! I'm staying put in La Florida's radioactive atmosphere for a super long time.

Dieting

A NY TIME I SUCCEED at not indulging in a mighty fine sweet treat, I ask myself, "Why wasn't I born in Florence, Italy, in the mid 1400's?" I could have worked for or dated Sandro Botticelli and my life would have been picture perfect." (Pun intended.) I could be as round as I liked. No problem with Tiramisu for breakfast, lunch, and dinner.

The whole problem with a diet is the diet. Did you ever notice that the first three letters of that ghastly word spell DIE? People think that they should skip meals in order to slim down but then when they do eat it's as if they turned into a tribe of starving Neanderthals at a meat festival. They splurge and end up gaining more weight because they unjustly deprived themselves. I just adore the delightful scientific fact that when you don't eat and think you are doing yourself a favor, your own body turns on itself and devours muscle.

How about the poor yo-yo dieters? They literally have less money than everyone because they purchased several different wardrobes: The OMG, I can't believe I'm this fat! I'm going on a diet tomorrow set of clothes; The holy crap, I look so good items that are never worn that long; The I'll buy this and that set of tops, slacks, shorts, and undergarments because I'll fit into those when I lose weight goodies; and the I can't even calculate the wages lost in the swimwear department category.

Who knew that the only way to succeed at losing weight, toning up, looking great, being healthy, and feeling confident is NOT to diet?

The gym trainers and Pilates/Yoga instructors ask, "Hello, life style changes, anyone?"

The vast majority of the American population replies, "Sorry, I can't hear you because of the loud crunch of these chips and fries we placed on our quarter pound beef patties. Don't worry though because it's all on whole wheat buns and we're gulping extra-large diet sodas."

Thank God grams of sugar and sugar alcohol content (What the heck *is* that anyway? Sounds enticing...) were not printed on all of our candies when we were growing up. Remember when the family dentist gave you a lollipop when you left the office? Counting calories, anyone? How about the endearing names of our favorite fattening delights: Sugar Daddy (the king of all confectioneries on a stick), Good and Plenty (Praise the heavens if you got your hands on a theater box.), Baby Ruth, Bit-O-Honey, Bubblegum Cigars and Cigarettes in come hither pastels, Chocolate Gold Coins, Pixy Stix (Poisonous straws which contain frightful doses of colorful tart sugar), those adorable Pez Candy Dispensers, and the ever popular Wax Bottles (filled with a diabetes-inducing disgusting syrup of unknown provenance). Even with all of those tasty toxins surging through our veins, we turned out alright—didn't we?

Traveling Solo

I KNOW I'M AN ANOMALY but I like to travel alone be it to the grocery store, downtown anywhere, across a country, or to an oasis in the middle of a desert. Think of all the possibilities knowing that there is no one to tell fibs to, make decisions for, or compromise with. You can do anything, at any time, with anyone. It's heaven on Earth but you have to keep your wits about you, at least most of the time. Personally, that bit of advice about thinking straight does not necessarily apply to the cost of the trip. I have often lost my grasp on reality regarding expenses but financially recovered by watching my pennies when I'm not livin' the dream.

One of my favorite legs of a trip is the airport itself. There are such interesting people in a wild variety of conditions: Completely exhausted from jet lag; unconscious; totally jacked up with excitement; depressed or crying; unbearably handsome or beautiful or both; mysterious and self-assured as in, "I only have carry-on luggage and I'm flying thousands of miles"; people who search the eyes of fellow travelers for someone to chat with; stylish dressers or those who couldn't care less and wear a hideous bathing suit and a sweatshirt; those who travel in the middle of the night or on popular holidays when the majority of humanity has already arrived at its destination; and individuals who feign disdain as their faces broadcast, "Don't even think about talking to me."

If I'm driving I prefer to depart at midnight because there are less insane drivers on the road. In my experience, truck drivers are polite, helpful, and responsible. They've guided me through snowstorms and kept me safe on the road. The most important lesson I've learned is to never allow my feathers to get ruffled if there is a delay of any kind. When I hear, "Sorry, your plane is cancelled." No problem. Do I really want to fly in an ice storm or monsoon that has crippled airports? Do I have a desire to go down in a burning ball of fire because mechanics were rushed? I don't think so. I honestly believe if there is a crimp in the itinerary, then for some reason, I'm not supposed to be travelling at that time. Fellow passengers have asked if they could purchase some of my sedatives during an overlay. No drugs are necessary. It's just a matter of preserving my brain cells and body.

How about travelling to a country such as Egypt when the State Department writes and calls begging you not to go? I'm packing twice as fast because the number of tourists just decreased from untold thousands to me and about a dozen other people. Don't get me wrong. I do arrange for assistance during my adventures but my helpers and guides need to be citizens of the culture I am visiting. As long as my intuition tells me that I'm not going to get hacked into little pieces, I'll gladly hire an eight-fingered driver in Mexico or go out to dinner with a chief of police in Italy. Let's ride those chubby little ponies in Iceland, gallop on horses along the beaches on the coast of Ireland, and get bumped around on the back of a terrified elephant in Nepal. The way I figure it, stardust to stardust; you only die once and my obituary would have a certain flare to it.

Failure

EVEN JEFF BEZOS, THE BILLIONAIRE founder and CEO of Amazon.com, Mother Theresa, Frank Sinatra, the Pope, and virtually everyone you ask, have considered themselves to be failures—sometimes at the peak of their careers. Just pick up a random biography of an entrepreneur, a movie star, a writer, or famous singer. How about the plumber who finally thought it best to become an electrician and now he's making more money than us. I would love to date one of those rich contractors who failed algebra in high school. What's the point of failure? If you're lucky, it will kick your ass into gear, and convince you to pick yourself up off the floor and try again. I don't think there would be a world as we know it if there weren't big time failures.

What about the cave people? Did they all say, "I'm not going to rub these freaking flints together any longer! Screw this, uncooked meat isn't that bad. So, a few of us die. There are worse things than maggots." Did Michelangelo complain that his back and arms hurt to the extent that he was going to call it quits on The Sistine Chapel? How many overnight successes worked their butts off for untold years?

Think about it. There's a solid truth delivered by T. H. Palmer's poem, "Try Try Again." If you failed spelling tests, math quizzes, or both, I hope a peer or an older loved one helped you study through those bugbears. I temporarily lost 60 percent of my hearing in sixth grade from diving and swimming. No one but my friends believed me or came to my aid. They helped me study and pass those paralyzing examinations. The ear, nose, and throat specialist my mom begrudgingly dragged me to scolded her and my teachers for not heeding my claims of deafness. I have to admit that I was perversely pleased that the tables were turned on my parent and so-called guardians.

Most importantly, I learned lifelong lessons to never give up; someone will always come to the rescue if you are brave enough to ask for guidance; and even after multiple tries, you can succeed. There's a clincher though. There may be a deeper reason for your failure. You may have made a choice that wouldn't be most beneficial to you. You have to be willing to change your course and be flexible. Thank God my lack of dried reeds and coordination brought my desire to be a professional basket weaver to a grinding halt. Just when you think you have it all figured out, you haven't. Hello, Circle of Life. What did you say? Oh, yes, I've heard that somewhere before, "Try, try again."

Fear

THANK YOU FOR MEETING with me for an interview. Kindly tell me about yourself, Fear.

Well, you've certainly met my little sister, Anxiety, and my oldest brother, Failure. I'm a middle child and a fraternal twin, I might add.

Can you tell me about your parents?

Of course, I'd be pleased to brag about my sources of inspiration. Everyone has become an acquaintance of or a downright pal with my dear ol' mom, Depression. My bigger than life father, Paranoia, has always been the black sheep of the family but we still love him. How can I forget grand pappy, Horror, and our favorite grandma on my mother's side, Panic? We rarely see my paternal grandparents, Dread and Alarm. They're always whining about something.

Since you're the focus of this interview, can you tell us a bit more about yourself, Fear?

No problema; I'm my biggest fan and, boy, do I have a following. Like every emotion, I've evolved over time. I mean I really got into that primeval fight-or-flight response situation. It depends on the individual species, whether you're going to run like hell or wait around and get your head torn off. I'll tell you one thing. Those humans certainly have a hard time deciding which one of my family members they like best.

Are you afraid of anything, Fear?

Just fear itself. Pun intended. Thank you, FDR and Thoreau.

Is there anything you'd like to add about yourself, Fear, so we can really get to know you?

Well, no sibling rivalry here. I'm an enthusiastic admirer of my twin, Terror. There's just something about getting the spinal cord and hormones involved that blows my mind.

Would you like to add a special message to your ever growing fan base, Fear?

I want to make it perfectly clear that I'm not all bad. A healthy dose of me can force you to finally apply for that promotion, ask out that hot neighbor, or write the sequel to the screenplay that no one's picked up. A little bit of me can go a long way.

Well, I have to say, Fear, this has been an eye-opening conversation. I was a little, how can I say, fearful, to sit down and have a chat with you.

Hey, that's my career, to scare the crap out of anyone or anything at any time. I'm only doing my job. I'm sure I'll be seeing you around sometime soon.

Dogs

THERE'S NOTHING LIKE the unconditional love of a dog when you walk in your front door. The happiness that exudes from every pore of your pet is like taking a shower in endorphins, those beloved hormonal mood elevators that are produced when you exercise. It's so much easier and pleasant to stroke your prancing companion than going to the gym. Plus, you don't have to pay your pooch those pesky fees.

During the course of your busy day perhaps you've committed seven armed robberies, stolen candy from defenseless children, ate nine pieces of cake when you swore you'd start another diet, or taken yet another undeserving sick day from work and went to the movies. You could be sound asleep, playing outside, or puking. No matter how you feel or act, Tippy, your trusty canine companion, will remain by your side. (Tippy is the name I call every dog that I don't know. It could be a yapping Chihuahua or a drooling St. Bernard.)

Lulu, the love of my life, is an adopted toy poodle. As I drive, walk around, or bicycle in my hometown with her, I simply adore watching grown men being led by their tiny treasured Yorkshire Terriers and little old ladies walking their cherished fierce German Shepherds. It's especially heartwarming to see an elderly person in a golf cart, not with a set of golf clubs, but next to a content bow-wow with its ears flapping in the wind. I have witnessed dogs calm down and soothe adults and children when those humans could be compared to members of a tribe of Terminators. If I'm in a nasty mood or something ridiculous has upset me, I often reflect upon J. W. Stephen's memorable quote, "Be the person your dog thinks you are!"

Ponder for a moment all of the money pet owners spend on grooming alone. When Lulu gets spruced up, it costs about the same as my hairdresser appointment. It's like I have a young, short, and furry child that has to look good so she's not a poor reflection on me. I wish my job's medical, dental, and vision insurance covered my dog. I could have purchased a Ferrari with all of the money I've spent on our family's last two extended family members. Don't even talk to me about food, pee pads (Thank baby Jesus for them!), treats, vitamins, toys, and outfits. (Yes, Lulu loves to wear her turquoise blue, chenille, turtle neck for those brisk Florida winter evenings.) Let's just buy stock in PetSmart and we'll be able to retire early.

Although I adore dogs, I'm a dedicated supporter of all members of the Kingdom Animalia. God bless strays and other unfortunate animals. I wish I could give every one of them a good home. In the morning you'll find me at my computer clicking away on TheAnimalRescueSite.com. I'm grateful this compassionate organization provides half a bowl of free food for a hungry animal with each simple movement of my index finger. Dogs, cats, wolves, horses, I don't care; let's feed as many of them as possible. Now, that's what I call progress that I can literally put my finger on.

Stress

EVERYONE SEEMS TO HAVE the same old gripe these days, "I'm SO stressed out!" Unlike fear, I don't see an upside to stress; greetings to you: acne, high blood pressure, depression, crime, and weight gain. I am envious of the lucky few who actually lose weight when they're hassled.

If you think about it, stress has probably been around as long as fear. It had to be anxiety producing to arrive home only to wonder if a cave bear was going to shred your family. "Hey, honey, let's take the kids for a walk. On second thought, we'd better not. That saber-toothed tiger looked pretty ornery yesterday."

It's not as if Neanderthals could hop on down to the deli for a picnic lunch. What if there weren't enough wooly mammoths to go around? "Hey, Wilma, I'm really starving. Let's eat Barney and Bamm-Bamm!" Cannibalism had to cause some tension. I'd be worried if I could become someone's main course. Nothing like your neighbors turning into possible predators to get the old ticker pumping too fast.

Even kids are tense due to the incredibly high and ridiculous expectations of the Common Core curriculum. Heck, I'm a teacher and I can't even solve some of the lower elementary math problems. Today's arithmetic quizzes aren't similar to the ones we were subjected to years ago. They involved pure computation with a starred word problem tagged on at the end for the brainiacs. Now, it's all about "multi-step real world word problems" such as, "If an

African bush elephant weighs approximately 12,000 pounds and a starving pride of lions eats part of it, how old will your Uncle Charlie be in the year 2048?"

The older students are super stressed because they have to deal with computerized math exams. What kills me is the verbiage. "Choose ALL possible answers to the problem." That means you have to solve parts A, B, C, D, E, and F to be sure you picked the correct answers. No wonder some pupils say, "Forget this; I'm not going to pass. I'm just going to Christmas tree in the answers on my Scantron." Let's double the stress factor after school. Family members, guardians, sitters, and counsellors can rarely help kids with homework. Even if adults had the time or inclination to do so, they can't figure out how to complete the assignments. I know folks who have threatened to leave town when Mathematics/Science Fair Projects were due.

Our government has finally realized that our educational system, well, sucks. What a surprise that young Americans aren't successfully competing with Asian students. Some of the major problems with schools these days besides the insane stress producing testing schedules are the unrealistic standards that increase annually and the fact that the curricula changes often. It's impossible to gather data to see what if anything is succeeding. Tests are approximately two years above the students' natural rate of intellectual development. You needn't test young children's capitalization and punctuation skills when they're learning how to hold a pencil. I challenge your everyday American grownup to pass any 5th grade math or science test.

Modern times have produced special types of mental, emotional, and physical stress. Foreign journalists complain about the tension caused by American presidential campaigns. I heard a BBC reporter groan that she couldn't bear the thought of the next round of American elections and that was just after Obama had begun his second term. If correspondents criticize those endless streams of vicious TV commercials, what about the trauma and stress they cause us when all we want to do is cuddle up to the boob tube and vegetate?

I have the highest respect for and publicly thank police officers, paramedics, and fire fighters for risking their lives on a daily basis. Imagine the stress they endure not to mention their families. How about the jobs and organizations that had to be created because of terrorism? Thank you, NCTC (National Counterterrorism Center.) It's stressful enough to travel by air after packing and getting to the airport eight hours earlier than your flight. Now, we have to deal with the aggravation of no water bottles passed certain checkpoints, endless lines, cavity searches, pat-downs, x-rays, and armed soldiers and militia strolling around giving everyone the evil eye.

Let's think about the high levels of stress for generations to come. Overworking is a common source of stress. Multitudes of people are holding down more than one job in an attempt to make ends meet. No luxuries there. Teens drop out of school to scrape out a living which produces yet another cycle of stress and poverty. Even writing this piece (which is my second job) has got me stressed out. Think I'll take an anti-depressant, study some math, and have a piece of cake with a chaser of bourbon.

Intuition

WHAT THE HECK WOULD we do without intuition? Wait, I know. We'd have accidents all the time; kill each other; cry constantly; and make the wrong decisions. In life you have to make the right choices and know how to handle different people and situations in a split second. Intuition is a lot more than having a well-developed intellect. You don't acquire this sixth sense without observing, listening, living, and getting burned (literally and figuratively.) Getting knocked down, dusting yourself off and getting up again, travelling around the world or exploring every corner of your 'hood, having your heart broken into tiny pieces, and plain old growing up are some of the best ways to develop intuition. Without it, you are dead in the water.

Intuition, in a way, predicts the future. Its experience and knowledge wrapped up together which allows you to sense the potential benefits or detrimental aspects of a set of circumstances. Street smarts is a type of intuition and much more than common sense. Let's see. It's 3:00 in the morning and you are drunk as a skunk. Should you accept a ride from a quartet of drooling meth addicts wearing sunglasses? Turn and talk. What about putting all your eggs in one basket? I don't care if you really are a chicken farmer who is actually considering putting all that hard work on the line or an average Joe thinking about investing your life savings in a too good to be true stock. Newsflash: If something is too good to be true, run for the hills with your wallet.

I recently received an automated message from my city government warning me to hang up if the IRS calls and threatens me with jail unless I purchase some weird items with my credit card; really? A quick analysis of this phone message would result in my saying two words to my caller and they wouldn't be Merry Christmas. Speaking of scam artists and predicting the future, who comes to mind? That's right, fortune tellers and their infamous crystal balls. They have balls for sure. They also possess tons of intuition. They can read your mind. Not really. They read your body language and are excellent listeners and scrutinizers. And for heaven's sake, stay clear of Ouija boards. They'll scare you to death.

It may sound sentimental but I think one of the best ways to aid the development of intuition is to heed the average parent's advice. "Please don't date that person because you'll probably end up with herpes at the very least and be clinically depressed until graduation." Of course, you didn't listen and neither will your kids but think of all the misery it would have saved everyone. Plus, wouldn't it be great to have not heard as many I Told You So's? Unfortunately, blunders are inevitable but vital in developing intuition. Alexander Pope's famous lines of poetry come to mind, "To err is human; to forgive, divine." Be merciful with yourself and others when intuition seems to have flown the coop because "Fools rush in where angels fear to tread." (I couldn't resist.)

Photographs

A PERSONAL PRACTICE has always been to never leave behind written, recorded, or photographic evidence of any kind. Don't even bother asking. My answer will begin with the words, "It will be a cold day in hell before …." I believe my feelings towards photographs began when I started travelling during those precious moments called breaks from teaching. I developed two rules for myself when I packed. I allowed myself to bring only one mother of a suitcase which I had to be able to maneuver independently and no cameras. My second dictum flabbergasted people almost as much as the fact that I rarely use my cell phone. Friends actually purchased disposable cameras for me to take on trips. I carefully nestled them between towels in the linen closet before my departure.

In my humble opinion, postcards are much better than photographs. They are sturdier than snapshots. Plus, you don't have to view strangers who are standing in front of a favored site or waste precious time focusing when you could be exploring. Fellow sightseers were often stunned when I appeared without a camera. I've received heaps of photos and email attachments from sympathetic tourists who felt my memory bank was a poor substitute for a Kodak Moment captured on film or a cell phone. I'm grateful for their generosity.

I've been in Brazil on the Amazon River in a dugout canoe in a state of awe only to be stupefied by a holidaymaker who struggled to balance himself because he was tenderly carrying an infant. The babe in arms turned out to be a camera lens dressed in swaddling clothes. He could've been a giant hors d'oeuvre for a school of piranhas if he fell into those murky waters. I've observed adults lose their senses in Ecuador's Galapagos Islands because they dropped their enormously expensive cameras in the water as they ran for their lives when they got too close to seemingly dormant sea lion bulls. Was risking life and limb and their sacred camera worth that stunning shot? Hmmm...

I despise having my picture taken. Yet, I'm the first one to grab a prop and smile. The best trick I've learned is to advise any photographer to count to three before freezing my image. Just remember to blink on two and then you won't look like a sleeping orangutan on three. Why not just leave the frigging camera home? Don't even get me started on selfies. OMG, conceited much? Everyone is turning into Kim Kardashian. Now, that's a reason not to get up in the morning.

Extinction

O N INNUMERABLE OCCASIONS new acquaintances and old friends have offered their condolences regarding the fact that I am an only child. Evidently, siblings can help absorb, counteract, redirect, or demystify the bizarre behavior of parents. I've found that loved ones, other than family members and even strangers, can provide the same service. People are also dismayed when they discover that I don't have forty-three cousins and are downright concerned that I haven't reproduced. I cheerfully explain, "I can't miss something I've never had." One Spanish lady remarked, "Oh, my poor woman, who will take care of you when you're old?" Quite frankly, I am elated I don't have to deal with the emotional nonsense and petty jealousies that darn near everyone on the planet grapples with every day.

I guess those are some of the reasons I never questioned why my dad rarely spoke of his relatives. It was as if he had hatched out of a solitary egg in the desert. My father shared only a handful of stories about his youth. I heard about adolescent high jinks such as when he and a chum sat in the backseat of his father's sedan with a loaded rifle. They took turns shooting holes through its roof. It was a miracle that the boys weren't blinded, deafened, or killed. Grandpa never punished them for this dangerous escapade. He simply had the car repaired. What was Grandpa waiting for; a friendly grenade in the glove box?

My maternal grandfather never uttered a word about his family in Ireland. His wife showed me a photograph of my German great grandmother. She looked like a portly vicious gun moll that beat puppies for a hobby. I thanked God that her weighty nasty bones were deep in the ground near Heidelberg. Grandma told me a few ghastly stories about how her younger sister died of consumption after not toweling off after a swim. She also introduced me to her single skinny brother, Uncle Willy. He smoked himself to death in no time at all. That was the extent of knowledge I gleaned of my family history on my mother's side.

At a young age I accepted the reality that the vast majority of my kin were either six feet under, totally nuts, not worth pursuing, or not interested in my existence. It never bothered me in the least. I actually cherish the peace and quiet of it all. Who cares if I die alone? We all do even if we take our last breath at the Macy's Thanksgiving Day Parade.

My mother told me I practically worried her to death on many occasions. As an educator I am blessed to have some time to travel. Dad always lived vicariously through me. Mom was scared spit less every time I set off for a foreign country until I arrived home. During her final days she recommended that I continue living my independent dreams because she never had the courage to do so. Ma offered her special brand of motherly advice, "You don't ever have to get married. If you do, be sure to marry someone who loves you more than you love him." I thought this was a rather callous but astute remark and silently stored the information with a few thousand grains of salt.

Today, I sit here with my crate of salt and am as free as a bird. Everyone who I cared about in my family has passed. I have no kids and I married a poodle. I'm one of the happiest people I know. Let's raise a glass to extinction. Cheers!

Friendship

NOW THAT WE ARE solidly entrenched in the Age of Technology, e-mails spewing remedies to life's difficulties float freely amongst computers. Many anonymous philosophical essays relating to friendship and love resurface year after year. Some of the messages are poignant and should be taken to heart. Yet, many of these poetic thoughts conclude with a warning that Beelzebub will pay your loved ones a visit if you don't forward them to forty-six individuals within twelve seconds. Such threats dampen even the most humorous, inspiring, or consoling communications.

I believe that everything happens for a reason so I painstakingly read every memo that is sent to me via cyberspace. One of the most insightful dispatches I received offered an explanation as to why each person we meet should be given serious consideration. This nugget of information covers married couples, families, friendship, lovers, one-night stands; you name it. A modern day nameless sage of the almighty internet wrote People Come into Your Life for a Reason, a Season, or a Lifetime. I believe that's true. Think of your best buddies. I have some pals that I've known since kindergarten as opposed to shall we say, a summer romance, or that forbidden make-out scene in sixth grade never to be spoken of again.

Keep in mind that relationships are different in this modern era. Ever so brief lustful alliances often lead to dating which has resulted in matrimony. (Talk about a lifetime sentence.) I believe that no one should be allowed to marry before they've dated for a minimum of five years. Then, and only then, an application for a license to reproduce would be considered. Not a single human could further populate this planet until the age of forty. No couple is smart enough to raise kids before that ripe old number and they haven't been friends long enough anyway. Today, couples divorce if one of them neglects to turn on the coffee maker in the morning. Friendships and marriages crumble because Harry slept with Sally, Shaniqua, the UPS guy, and, Vivienne and Fred. The possible convolutions are many and not for the faint-hearted.

Let's face it, friendship can be as fragile as a butterfly or as sturdy as an oak. It can be the best thing in the world or it can fragment your heart into teeny-weeny pieces. Sometimes you can't collect all of those smithereens ever again but, fortunately, more friends are waiting to be made.

Parking

A<small>S A TREMBLING TEEN</small> my dad taught me all of his parking tricks in order to pass my driving test. He also made me careen down highways to the trafficy tip of New York City on a Saturday afternoon. Meanwhile, I had only driven around our block in peaceful suburbia a few times. We were in an Oldsmobile Cutlass whose tires had no traction. If I hit a pebble, it changed lanes. By the time we returned from The Big Apple, my hands were paralyzed. Perhaps those were the frightened seeds which blossomed into the utmost confidence in my ability to park. If it's scientifically feasible for a car to fit into a space in any weather condition, I will park it. Buddies and strangers even ask me to park their cars for them.

Parking in Manhattan and its surrounding boroughs calls for practice, talent, a basic understanding of physics, ESP, good fortune, and *coraggio*. I can hone in on an empty space at midnight on a weekend in Greenwich Village the way a seasoned hound dog sniffs out a corpse. Parking in places like the horizontal state of Florida is simply not challenging even if you are hogtied and blindfolded behind the steering wheel or subjected to an art fair in Delray or one of those rousing Saturday nights in Miami.

A healthy portion of cojones is vital when it comes to a parking stand-off especially if you are speeding towards a space on a northerly course and your nemesis is in reverse with intent to kill in a southerly direction. You have to be willing to risk life, limb, and a mammoth increase in your car insurance for a secure space in the

Asphalt Netherworld. A good deal of sneering, waving of fingers, and the cursing of ancestors may also be involved.

There's nothing like coming home from a long day at work, circling the blocks in your neighborhood, and spotting a space which is one centimeter longer than your vehicle. Get ready to turn your steering wheel all the way in both directions a thousand times. In your head you hear a scathing voice snarl, "Round and round. Back up. Now round and round the other way. Inch forward and be careful about it. AGAIN; round and round; AGAIN. Stop crying, you baby! Don't you want to have dinner tonight and soak your sore muscles after this grueling exercise? Well, you better buck up, my delicate flower, and gently kiss, NOT DENT, any bumpers. There's no sense in turning back now. Oh, Lord, have mercy."

After all that exhausting effort, don't you just hate it when you finally crawl out of your car, mop the sweat from your brow, proudly limp to your front door, and glance back at your amazing feat of parking between two cars with the thickness of a dime's worth of air between them, only to see one of those dastardly vehicles drive off?

Imagine repeating that grueling parking process with half a dozen fractured ribs and a STICK SHIFT. I needed paramedics by the time the sun went down and I had successfully parked my blasted car. Let's reminisce what it's like to park on a hill in a car equipped with a manual transmission. Talk about sweating bullets but what an ingenious method of arm and leg toning, improving reflexes, and fulfilling those arduous cardio requirements. With enough parking, I could quit the gym altogether. What do ya say? Let's go for a drive.

Teaching

I'VE BEEN AN elementary school teacher for half of my life. I remember surviving rigorous Montessori trainings in Washington, D.C. My fellow housemates felt sorry for me because of the curricular expectations. They were Georgetown law students. Besides studying and creating teaching manuals in various subjects for two years, I worked three nights a week from midnight to 5:00 a.m. for the United Mine Workers Association filling out forms for people stricken with black lung disease. What joyous days they were. I carried on by repeating that old adage, "Whatever doesn't kill you makes you stronger."

I finally made it to my first day of classes with a group of three to five year olds. I politely introduced myself and was called Chlorine Sherbet for a week. Every time someone spoke my name I expected a bedazzled stripper to make an appearance. Yet, I was hooked because of the honor of seeing little ones gain emotional, social, and intellectual independence on a daily basis.

The good always outweighed the bad and there was plenty of bad. I recall a diminutive child named Maria with long black braids. She spun on the school's tire swing until streams of vomit encircled her. It looked as if an exorcism was taking place on the playground. I couldn't call her mother fast enough. Ah, yes, little Rebecca and her death wish. Every year on her birthday, the Beckster would have a horrible accident. I swore nothing would happen to her on my watch; wrong, Claudine. We were laughing and have a good ol' time during recess when she grabbed the fireman's pole, looked me straight in the eye, loosened her fingers on purpose, and jumped. A paramedic held her chin together as we sped up Broadway in an ambulance. I asked myself why this happened and eventually blamed the fact that BOTH of her parents were psychologists.

Tutoring young children, teens, and adults is another form of teaching after school. I love this one-on-one time. Unfortunately, I came to realize that the richer a parent was, the higher the checks bounced. Therefore, it became a cash and carry business for me. A babysitter, a parent, or an older sibling would wait in my apartment while I worked with my student. Money was transferred and then you'd get your kid back. I was adamant about not going to my charge's homes. Parents would suck extra time out of me no matter how often I said I had to stick to a strict schedule. Plus, I had to pay for transportation and time lost between jobs.

Some of my favorite students were Japanese mothers who didn't speak a word of English. They would arrive in the evening with a notebook and a tape recorder. I had a children's book called I SPY which contained a vast array of classified nouns. We'd spend one night in the kitchen. I'd hold different utensils such as a fork and say the word very clearly in English. The mom would write the Japanese word under the picture of the fork. I would then repeat the word into the recorder and she would say it in Japanese. There was a built-in control of error for each bit of vocabulary we studied. We'd progress to pieces of furniture, articles in the bathroom, means of transportation, and pieces of clothing. By the time the respectable lady departed, my flat would be littered with plates, cups, pots, pans, spoons, knives, brassieres, fishnet stockings, stilettos, slips, hats, gloves, boots, bathing suits, pants, suitcases, make-up, tissues, and toilet paper. We'd be giggling up a storm and eventually move on to basic verbs. In no time at all, my adult pupil was happily speaking broken English and using her husband's credit cards with reckless abandon.

Every day at school there is a multitude of rewards teachers receive from an unexpected hug or a nod of understanding to a smile of appreciation during that special moment when a child reads or computes independently or with less assistance. Of course, I'm thrilled when there is an increase in scores but I'm more interested in spotting a twinkle in a child's eye. It's like getting a sign of confirmation from the universe. Teaching is in my DNA; it keeps me on course.

Sickness

S ICKNESS CAN BE a good thing. Being ill is the body's way of saying, "Take it easy, you fool! Lie down. Sleep. Eat better. Don't worry so much. The world doesn't revolve around you. Take off a day from work." Even if you are the president of the United States of America, the vice president is right there to jump into your shoes. If my memory of social studies classes serves me right, the Speaker of the House would be chomping at the bit at that juncture. I'm guessing that the line of succession continues until the butler at the White House has total control of our government. The bottom-line is that no one is irreplaceable so, snuggle up next to a box of Kleenex, turn on the telly, and blow your nose as loudly as you can. Nobody cares!

Even if you're sneezing your brains out, you're always in a state of denial when that slight achiness begins. Your nose starts running intermittently and then the hacking starts. At that viral point, most people continue to blame their blossoming virus on an uncomfortable chair or cat dander before they admit they've been stricken with another case of the sniffles. If you tough it out, the sad truth is that it will take longer for you to regain your original strength by waiting for the weekend which will be ruined anyway.

When you're NOT sick but take one of those revered "mental health days," think of how great you feel after the initial guilt wears off after thirty-two seconds. You need some time to yourself even if it's not a scheduled holiday. Think of all the garbage we juggle on a daily basis. It's a miracle that we're all not on antidepressants simply from the anxiety caused by watching the nightly news. Everyone will need a DNR (do-not-resuscitate order) by the next inauguration. Until that woeful day, take a sick day and relax but don't tell my boss I said so.

Hope

WHAT IS HOPE ANYWAY; a feeling, an emotion, a namby-pamby untouchable thing? All I know is life would be an even sorrier state of affairs without it. Where would we be without hope even at the most mundane levels?

"Gee, I hope that Aunt Beatrice won't come to our wedding. She's a real boozer and won't shut up once she gets tanked."

"I'll just die if they're not serving after midnight. I hope they still have those cheesy fries!"

"I hope I pass that drug test next week. I really need this job. I only had two tokes a couple of weeks ago. It wouldn't be fair if they didn't hire me."

Hope is defined by Encarta Dictionary as a "confident . . . feeling that something desirable is likely to happen." Who was the genius who bottled the stuff and made it a legitimate thing? When did people start hoping; maybe in ancient Egypt? "I really hope and pray to the gods and goddesses that there's not another flood next year. Yeah, yeah, I know that after the Nile's water subsides the fields are more fertile. I'm just so sick of this soggy mess!"

Will people ever stop hoping? If they do, then we're really up the creek. Do animals and insects hope for anything? "I hope that her aim hasn't improved with that stinking fly swatter. My wing still hurts from last night. Cripes; here she comes again!"

Personally, I hope for something at least a dozen times a day. Even before I get my tired butt out of bed in the morning I hope that our crazy world won't blow up and everyone will be more tolerant of one another. Who doesn't hope that they can lose at least a quarter of a pound by next Saturday? Within an hour of arriving at school I'm hoping that little Joey won't smack big Esther again and that at least fifty percent of the kids did some homework last night. By midmorning on Mondays, the entire population of workers is hoping that the weather will be pleasant next weekend. Who hasn't hoped that their salary would magically increase and that the government would abolish all sales tariffs, interest rates, and income taxes?

You can't tell me that you haven't hoped that the retirement age would be lowered to 25 by 2020 and that all the utility companies would implode simultaneously. Hope has got to have squirmed its way into your soul every single time you turn on the news. "God, please let all this bitter lunacy cease and let us live in peace. You've just got to stop these bloodcurdling Chiller Theatre types of diseases from spreading because of contact with Martian-like mosquitoes." We've simply got to let almighty hope reign. (I just hope that I can cough up another idea for the next chapter.)

Love

THERE MUST BE A MILLION types of love. "I just love pizza; don't you?" "He's so hot! I simply love his abs." I surely love my dog. I know people who love their cats beyond comprehension. How about all those horse lovers? Hugs and kisses for Seabiscuit, Secretariat, and Man O' War. Animal lovers are everywhere and you're thrilled about that if you're a PetSmart stockholder.

Thank heavens for the love of our fellow men and women even though you'd doubt its existence if you ever picked up a newspaper or watched the idiot box. Let's not forget religious love, the marrying kind of love and its antithesis, adulterous love. I've heard individuals proclaim their love for their hairdressers, "I'd never leave him in a million years!" Not many would say that about their spouses.

Desire is often the precursor of love or confused with it at the very least. "We've been in lust for over a week now." How about puppy love? "I'm only fifteen years old and Jimmy is the love of my life. I'd die without him." Three weeks later, Ricardo appears on the scene and Jimmy is as good as expired yogurt.

"I'm a nature lover in spite of the bee stings, mud, and grass stains. It's fantastic to be in the fresh air. Could you pass me my inhaler, please?"

Hey, we're at a country club. "I love bridge, tennis, diamonds, and my vodka most of all. What's the new tennis pro's name?"

Well, hello, Wall Street. What did you say? "We love money, superficiality, and our egos!" That's what I thought you said.

There seems to be an abundance of patriotic love which is especially tested before, during, and after presidential elections. Listening to the endless debates filled with rhetoric and empty promises could cause the staunchest soldier to become a conscientious objector. I simply must include the famous slogan from the turbulent 1960's, "Make love, not war." I wish that motto was practiced more often.

How can we ignore the love of sports? The Super Bowl encompasses the love of advertising and big bucks as much as Americans' love of baseball and the rest of the world's love of soccer. Talk about mucho moolah for the players, owners, and corporations. How ya doin' NBA, Indy 500, and NASCAR lovers, bookies, and gamblers?

There's nothing quite like forbidden love, secret love, a first love, a lost love, and sorry to have to mention it, but unrequited love. Everyone's had a creepy crawly experience of obsessive love and I hope more than a dose of erotic love whatever your tastes may be. That brings us to baby love. A new mother's love of her infant borders on paranoid and psychotic behavior. Parents love their kids so much that they would lay down their lives for them. Toddlers love their thumbs even more. They suck them until there's a welt on those overly used joints. Don't get me started on a little one's love of a blankie. Many a tear has been shed when a beloved, stained, bacterial-laden, and shredded piece of cloth hits the washing machine for a long overdue cycle or two.

Ah, the love of music from Beethoven to The Beatles. Don't forget Nat King Cole, Madonna, and Reggae. You know that it's virtually impossible to wax on about love without at least one schmaltzy song title such as, "Love Makes the World Go 'Round."

Good God, what about the love of books which couldn't exist without the love of writing. "I love poetry, history, mysteries, biographies, satirical essays, plays, and crossword puzzles." Of course you do; you're a librarian.

Lastly, there are those little words that sound irresistible in every language and which human beings long to hear whether they admit it or not. Iway ovelay ouyay. *Je t'aime.* *Te quiero.* I love you. There, I said it.

If

WHAT'S THE WORST WORD in the English language? Yep, you guessed it; IF. Put WHAT and IF together and you have a recipe for potential disaster. What if I don't get accepted? What if she/he doesn't like me? What if I fail? What if I succeed? What if you just shut the hell up and give it a go? All they can say is a big fat, "No way, Jim Bob, go back to the drawing board." Maybe they'll laugh in your freaking face. You ask yourself, "How much rejection can a person take?" The answer is, "More than you can believe, my little missy." (Missy is an appropriate title for both genders at this point.)

I've thought about it for a long time. I believe that the problem behind every obstacle boils down to either fear or jealousy with a giant dose of IF thrown in for dramatic effect. What if I don't get accepted? See, you're scared AND thinking of someone who was already accepted. So, what does that prove? That I'm right, of course, but I don't want to make you feel worse. What if she/he doesn't like me? Well, others have probably preceded you and considering your personal timeframe, you could win the big prize or, at least be the next in a long line of successors. Just step up to the plate for God's sake.

Psychiatrists, therapists, and everyday authors have written books concerning this particular mental roadblock. Here's my take on the barrier. When it boils down to it, our anxieties fit into two categories. You'll be scared out of your wits to fail. OR, now try to

36

wrap your brains around this baby. You'll be needing loads of fresh underwear while you're debating about succeeding. How the heck can that happen; very easily, my "young grasshopper." In fact, one or the other scenarios has already acted itself out innumerable times in your life and you weren't even aware of it.

Don't let mommy or daddy, wife or hubby, relatives, co-workers, friends, lovers, allies, enemies, strangers, extraterrestrial forms of life, and most of all, yourself, convince you that you can't accomplish something. The concept of the ol' drawing board is real. Perhaps you will have to try, try again. (Wait, that rings a bell. I have to check my Table of Contents. Pages being turned are heard then silence. Okay, we're safe to carry on. This is a huge gray area in the human mind, a real foible.)

You CAN lose the weight, write that book, get your diploma, find a job, raise another kid, make more money, and find someone/ something to love you back. Newsflash: There are people doing all of those things right now and simultaneously. I know; they must be dating Dr. Phil and on crystal meth but, my point is that damn near anything can be accomplished. Just look around you and carpe diem to the max.

Parents

WATCHING MY FOLKS fade away was a difficult process. When I thought they couldn't hold on much longer, they'd come up for more air and carry on for another few years. The specters of sickness and dwindling funds continually haunted them. They never had an opportunity to save for a rainy day because they were too busy getting swindled or throwing a party.

On a whim my father decided to move from Connecticut to Florida in spite of my mother's poor health. It was bewildering to hear my parents apprise me of the fact that they were moving over one thousand miles away because, "There's nothing keeping us here." What a confidence building statement for an only child to hear and such a thoughtful gesture to notify me by phone. Not surprisingly, Claude and Claudine's move to Florida wasn't typical by any means. One would assume that older people such as my folks would take a cab or limousine to a New York airport and fly directly into Palm Beach. No, that would be too easy.

Mom detested flying so she convinced dad to drive to Florida. The only way I know how to get there is Interstate 95. However, my mother felt uncomfortable on I-95 because of the "gigantic speeding trucks." She insisted that they take an "alternate route." I was terrified as I visualized the possible scenarios which could evolve as my parents weaved their way through the Deep South. A weepy fond farewell was all I had after their departure for three days. In my mind's eye I saw them bludgeoned in the red clay of

Georgia, beaten senseless in North Carolina, and drugged and bound by sadists in Tallahassee.

Imagine my glee when more than seventy-two hours after our initial goodbyes my slightly tipsy mother called. I could barely hear her because of the sound of roaring engines in the background. I calmly inquired as to their location as I envisioned crazed motorcyclists ready to gang bang her as they forced my drooling father to watch. Somehow, someway, I swear to God, they were in a house of ill repute in South Amboy, New Jersey. My mother explained that they "drove and drove but couldn't figure out how to get to Florida." They finally decided to rest in a motel. There were no closets in their room. The perimeter of the ceiling "was decorated with blinking red cherry lights." The sound of engines was my dad "firing up the Jacuzzi." Mom stated that she "would never sit in that thing because every disease in the world probably lived in there." I envisioned my dad's genitalia shriveling with the most severe STD known to mankind.

As we once more said goodbye, ma gave me their latest travel update. They decided to hire an agent to map out their way to Florida. I simply stated that I loved them and prayed for their safety. Sometimes you just have to give up and hope for something a little less than total disaster.

Hangovers

WHY, WHY, WHY did I do this to myself again? Everyone who indulges in alcoholic beverages has learned that the number one rule for preserving liver and brain cells is NOT TO MIX DRINKS. Then, why pray tell, did I suck down two sakes during cocktail hour, some white wine, and to top it all off, red wine with dinner? I'll tell you why…because I was having a hilarious time. Good friends, great conversation, lots of laughter, delicious appetizers, a swell entrée, and just a bit of dancing to some fabulous tunes. Who could ask for more? I could. May I please have another Tylenol, some Rolaids, and another ten hours of sleep? Throw in a sick day from work and a promise never to do this to myself again.

Depending on the level of decadence of your teenage years, there were countless bouts of intoxication often accompanied by amnesia and vague promises of abstinence. Youthful vigor and immaturity have a habit of making the most sincere apologies to your battered body disappear by the next weekend. The joys of inebriation during high school pale in comparison to the blackouts through those college days of being a true lush only to be followed by teaming up with other alcoholics-in-training in the course of your "first apartment/first job/thank God I'm out of my family home" period.

The passing of time may or may not dampen your spirits. (Pun intended.) At all ages there will be raging soirees where you get carried away with the crowd. Some individuals often decide to stick with just beer or wine. I chose to switch to the delightful Japanese drink, sake. Who can resist a libation that can be served hot or cold in an adorable wooden box, glass vessel, or ceramic cup? Believe me, I did my research. Premium sake has no sulfites, additives, or preservatives which only add to the pain in my cranial cavity the next morning. Sake is simply fermented rice and water and has one-third of the acidity of wine. Did I hear a sincere thank you from my sensitive stomach lining? Sake also packs quite a punch; its alcohol content is roughly 20%. That's why two is my limit; well, most of the time. (That's also why beer drinkers keep on guzzling all day and night because most beer's alcohol content is from 3% to 9%. Check out the labels, bubba.)

There's only one drawback to my beloved sake. It's not served everywhere and, unless you know and love me, the general population doesn't keep a reserve of sake in the pantry. I solve this problem by bringing two darling frosted glass bottles of sake with me and a colorful straw. My sake fits comfortably within my handbag if I am attending an indoor event. If I'm outdoors at a gathering and wish to maintain an aura of respectability, I neatly wrap my petite decanter in a napkin, and voi-freaking-la, it appears that I'm sipping on ginger ale or some other pale cola.

In order to avoid nausea, groaning, unexplained bruises, hideous selfies, embarrassing memories, pound packing trips to McDonald's, a mysterious hole in your bank account, or a combination of all of the above, you have to make some choices. Unfortunately, you have to pick among sobriety, moderation, or self-discipline. I think I'll go with a mixture of moderation and self-discipline. What about you?

Writing

I LOVE TO WRITE just about anything: letters, lists, complaint forms, blogs, comments on surveys, vignettes, emails, proposals, and even a thesis or two. The concept of automatic writing is very real to me. Sometimes thoughts flood my mind. I begin to compile my ideas as fast as I can because they are streaming out of me. That's why I keep a small notebook next to my bed, in my purse, stuffed in the glovebox, and conveniently strewn about my home. I've heard about the curse of writer's block and pray that will never plague me. Fortunately, I'm a Gemini. It's as if I have twice the usual banter saturating my noggin.

Perhaps you noticed that I omitted texting in my string of various types of writing because I simply won't text. (Shudders of incredulity pulsate 'round the world.) Besides causing text claw, carpal tunnel syndrome, increasing rates of difficulty recognizing emotions when face-to-face with an actual human, alarming levels of rudeness, car accidents, mortalities, and what I refer to as a general affliction known as brain sucking, texting is also responsible for the lingering death of spelling, capitalization, punctuation, and grammar skills. God forbid that introductions, vivid supporting details, and conclusions are included unless you are sexting.

I think my desire to write somehow emerged during my sentence as a parochial elementary school student. Nuns were often a combination of nemesis and inspiration. In one class Sister Arthur would slug me for what she perceived to be an incorrect slant to my cursive letters. During the next period, Sister Loretta encouraged me to try my hand at poetry, narratives, and non-fiction. Opinions were rarely sought after by Catholic teachers but found their way into my diaries where they scorched a hole in many a page.

Writing is communication whether it is an exchange between friends or lovers, a Nobel Prize winning document of international importance, or a forbidden note on a scrap of paper exchanged in middle school. The children, adolescents, and adults of every nation have a right to literacy so they can bestow that learned gift upon the generations to come. So, please, cut down on the texting; we have to lead by example.

Character

I WORK WITH ELEMENTARY aged children. It's my job to support them and to attempt to get them to think about their attitude, behavior, and speech. There's a paper weight on my desk which is one of the best presents I've ever received. A previous principal gave this token of appreciation to every faculty member at the first big meeting of the year. I guess she wanted to set a certain tone. It's made by a company called The Education People, Inc. and reads, "Character is what you say or do when no one else is looking." (Please spread that tidbit of knowledge forevermore.)

On any given day there are many soul-searching questions I ask myself such as, "Why did THAT happen; perhaps a lack of character?" Think of all the times you spotted careless slobs dump garbage from their cars. I almost crashed in a fit of rage when one loser threw pieces of chicken out of his window on a highway ramp. Greasy thighs, legs, and wings bounced off my hood and windshield. How about your friendly pickpockets, embezzlers, thieves, drug lords, and my favorite, "he told me to do it" moron? Why not throw in some stock brokers (Bernie Madoff, Jordan Belfort, Ivan Boesky), greedy corporations (Exxon, Halliburton, BP), and politicians? (There's too many to list.) Where were these people when lessons regarding the development of character were being discussed and taught, The Sociopaths' Institute of Criminal Intentions?

The nuclear family is in the throes of death throughout our

world. Character is learned from modeling, verbal cues, and lectures as a child matures. It doesn't matter who that "rock" is in your life. It could be a grandma, an older brother, an aunt who raises you, a caring neighbor, or a parent if you're lucky enough to have at least one of them. Count your blessings if you had two parents who tried their best. Kids need strict boundaries and they appreciate it when someone cares enough to say, "Greetings, I don't think so. We need to talk."

What does character mean to you?

"That plumber is honest. He never overcharges for parts or labor."

"Love oozes out of that mother. If I had five kids under ten years of age, I'd tear my hair out."

"You can really trust that accountant. I've gotten a chunk of change for my return each year and I know the IRS won't come after me."

"My kid's teacher is a saint. She's strict but fair and her students respect that."

"If there's one thing I can't tolerate, it's a liar. I truly love him because he's always told me the truth."

"His wife has been ill for the last ten years. He's taken care of her each and every day. What a faithful and compassionate guy."

"She lost her job last year but has held on to the house. Working two or three jobs just to make ends meet; talk about fortitude."

"They've been married for fifty-four years. I'm sick of dating after a few weeks. That's what I call devotion."

Long story short, character is plain old backbone as my dad used to say. How are your vertebrae holding up?

Games

I LOVE GAMES! Not mind games with your boyfriend who claims he's not cheating or the kind that James Bond plays with SPECTRE agents but real games. Remember Twister? Hello, sex with your clothes on. Whether you're in your living room or a casino, add some snacks and liquid refreshments, and you're in for a memorable time. From Go Fish, gin rummy, canasta, bridge, solitaire, craps, roulette, Monopoly, Scrabble, Backgammon, checkers, chess, Charades!, to Jenga; all of these games have provided untold millions with unadulterated fun.

"Let's go bowling!"

"I'd rather play tennis with Eddie while mom and dad play miniature golf."

"Now I can't figure out who to hang with."

Everyone has their favorite games. Do you want to play a solitary game of Rubik's Cube? Kill me now. I'll never be able to figure it out. I did adore playing games with my grandmother. God bless her. Parcheesi was a mind-numbing board game with dice and little wooden men who tried their best to get home as fast as possible... nine hours later. Give me Candy Land any time.

"Anyone for a whirlwind round of Mouse Trap?"

"Did someone suggest a game of tag?"

"Oh, I prefer Hide-and-Seek. Can't wait another second; I'll even count to one hundred and try to find you. Now, skedaddle!"

"Come on; let's play Hide-and-Seek in the water with Marco Polo." (Splashing is heard.)

"Marco"

"Polo"

"Speak louder, you cheater."

"Marco"

"POLO!"

What's so great about games? They take your mind off reality. Who gives a darn about the overdue mortgage payment when you've got a bean bag in your hand? I can't even think of my outrageous property tax statement when I'm a little tipsy and aiming a dart. Recall those fabulous ancient games that people of all ages are addicted to like soccer, bocce ball, and horseshoes. I'd be remiss if I didn't mention more modern favored games like croquet, baseball, football, and basketball. Give me a few kids, a pencil, and a piece of paper. We'll have a grand time AND I'll teach them some spelling and vocabulary tips when they beg me to play Hangman again. Will they ever tire of playing Heads Up 7 Up? Will I ever tire of playing Heads Up 7 Up or Four Corners? I hope not.

Who wants to play Dress Up? Whether you're four or forty-four, you can't deny the pleasure of becoming your alter ego or someone's dream lover. It's like having Halloween every day of the week. Some of the best games I ever played were the ones I made up myself or with a few pals. It doesn't matter where you are when you're a kid with an imagination. Just gather a table, a few blankets, some pillows, and see what unfolds. You won't get out of a treehouse if you're lucky enough to find one. Nothing fancy is ever really needed. A tree with thick branches to climb on will supply endless hours of pure merriment. Sandcastles on the beach, hiding under a tipped over canoe, building a fort; I'll never forget those games that Mother Nature gave us free of charge.

No one is ever too old to play games and if you think you are, whisper to yourself, "Marco…Polo" and maybe a few esteemed memories will resurface.

Travel Tips

I T'S FUNNY WHAT STICKS in your head when you're travelling. I
found no truer advice than the warning, "Do NOT enter a tour
boat's kitchen when sightseeing in China." You'll die of starvation
if you do. Let's just say I never imagined so many uses for a shower
and showering wasn't one of them. After I peeked, I only drank
bottled beer and ate rice that afternoon.

Lazy Susans are utilized even in the most stylish restaurants in
the Orient. I was mystified by an ever present wooden bowl on a
revolving tray which contained marble sized balls of what appeared
to be white Wonder Bread. I was advised to swallow a few if I
choked on the bones of the fish entrées. Evidently, deboning is not
a refined culinary art in parts of the East. The doughy pellets force
pesky spiny obstacles down one's trachea. Voilà! You're alive when
dessert arrives.

At times it is necessary for thrill-seeking travelers to fly in
military planes that are not equipped with the luxury of pressurized
cabins. Such aircraft are fitted with rustic seats which line the
interior of the fuselage. Heavy cargo, crates of food, and luggage are
stored in the tail of the plane and are clearly visible to all passengers.
Tiny windows are so far above eye level that they provide minimal
light. The seat belts look like they were recruited from a garbage bin
after needy soldiers were provided with something more efficient
to hold up their pants.

It is standard procedure on such planes for a wicker basket

filled with dingy cotton balls of questionable origin to be circulated amongst an assorted cast of characters. Initially, I couldn't figure out what the white fluffy orbs were used for so their tattered straw container left my hands quicker than a deployed hand grenade. I also didn't see the necessity of tightening my security harness until my eyes bulged out of their sockets; silly me.

I discovered that a gradual take-off is not generally practiced in such airborne vehicles. On one occasion in the heart of South America, I felt as if I unwittingly participated in a rocket launch. I was positive that my eardrums were shattered when we shot into the atmosphere. My body was catapulted through the main aisle of the aircraft and landed in a pile of army supplies. I was dazed but managed a girlish smile as either horrified or apathetic faces glanced at my crumpled figure. I didn't dare move until I was sure that the plane had leveled off. When I returned to my empty seat, I strapped myself in like a deceased buck on top of a Land Rover and stuffed enough cotton in each ear to fill a teddy bear. This is a cautionary tale. Tighten your seat belt for God's sake and if someone hands you cotton on an airplane, be sure to take it.

Quite a few of my days in East Africa began long before the sun rose. My extravagant tent was better equipped than most homes. It was raised about two feet above the ground and had polished slate floors, roomy closets, modern plumbing, and electrical conveniences. Each morning, hot chocolate was delivered to my abode before I began my explorations. However, there were a few unique requirements regarding the upkeep of my well-being. I had to zip up my home each night and tie a slew of double knotted bows to ensure that I wasn't mauled by curious and hungry baboons. After dinner, I had to walk briskly to my sleeping area with a flashlight. I was warned to listen for any sounds behind me because there was a chance that I'd be attacked and eaten by wild cats. No worries; I adored every minute of my time in the jungle.

Staving off the heat in the evenings was a priority because there was no air conditioning in our flat in Rome. After a scrumptious meal at one of the many excellent trattorias in the neighborhood, we'd sit and laugh in a blissful state until the wee hours of the morning. The Italians were amazed by my remedy to keep us cool. Night after night I placed my hosts' and their guests' feet and forearms in pots and pans filled to the brim with cold water and a few ice cubes. Sighs of delight and relief lingered in the air as bottles of wine were passed. After I departed, my low cost method of chilling broiling bodies continued into the fall.

I was the driver whenever we travelled in Italy. Hours were spent speeding along the Autostrada which makes Interstate 95 look like a kiddy ride at Disney World. The legal speed limit is approximately 81 mph for cars. There were always people who found the pace too slow. When I made the error of not getting out of their way fast enough, they repeatedly flashed their headlights and rode my back fender until they were practically in the trunk.

One afternoon my Fiat's stick shift disengaged itself. I turned to my friends, waved the broken car part in the air, and calmly announced, "We're going to die." Screams and nervous laughter engulfed us as I held the steering wheel with one hand and frantically screwed the gearshift back into place with the other. Naturally, we repeatedly toasted our survival that night. We were thankful that we didn't make the evening news as the latest fiery heap of metal on that notorious freeway.

Alas, my travelling days came to a standstill when my folks decided to move down south. I rarely considered flying to The Sunshine State as a sought after pleasure trip. My parental visits became a routine that transformed into an obligation which I felt was my karmic duty to fulfill. It turns out that every one of my journeys whether they were to Seville, Spain, or Atlantis, Florida was an intricate part of my destiny. Oddly enough, I didn't really mature into a full-fledged adult until I experienced life in Palm Beach County, USA.

Waiting

WAITING IS AS COMMON as breathing in today's society in spite of all our modern gadgets. The dentist's waiting room will always be filled with forlorn clients dreading the drill. The veterinarian's office will still be chocked-full of shaking puppies and mewing cats clawing their owners. Unless you go grocery shopping and complete your errands in the late hours of the night like I do, you're going to be stuck in a few lines. Doing what? Yup; waiting. How many times have you listened to someone say, "Now, just wait a minute!"

"Wait for me, PLEASE!"

"Kindly be seated in the (dreaded) Waiting Room."

"Good heavens, do I have to wait in another queue?"

"Have you read Waiting for Godot lately? Talk about eternal waiting."

Traffic delays will surely make you wait. Just thank God you don't live in Kenya or China where jams can last as long as 3 to 12 days. Vendors may have been ecstatic but everyone else must have contemplated moving to the Western Hemisphere. Who can forget the 10-mile-long metal nightmare on the New York Thruway caused by the Woodstock Festival? (I was in it.) A much more significant traffic jam was caused by the falling of the Berlin Wall when approximately 18 million cars were on the roadway between East and West Germany. I'm sure many families' eardrums are still scarred with the words, "Are we there yet?"

Let's ponder the wait time in airports or as I have nicknamed them, implosion centers. How many times in countries throughout the world have passengers gone berserk because Mother Nature made them wait? The air traffic controllers, pilots, and stewards have no control over nor'easters, hurricanes, whiteouts, blackouts, terrorism, or any other concoction of events that cancel flights. So, what do you do at the airport if your flight does not arrive or depart on time? That's correct; you wait.

Is there a purpose to waiting? Well, yes. Most importantly, the waiting time during gestation and metamorphosis results in new life. Fertilized eggs and seeds keep the world chugging along as we know it. One of life's major lessons is learning how to wait without cursing, leaving in a huff, pounding something or someone, or making a general ass out of yourself. There's only one remedy to the ever-present problem of waiting. It's a magical solution which is often absent in the DNA make-up of most Americans. Have you guessed what it is? After 10,985,274 tries, multiple sighs, and hints, a mere fraction of U.S. citizens respond in a tentative and confused whisper, "Patience?"

I was born and bred in a suburb of New York City and currently reside in South Florida. Practicing patience has been a lifesaver for me. I was told by a nurse who helped me with my parents that it would take two full years to get used to the pace of the South. I can testify to the veracity of that statement. EVERYTHING takes longer in Turtlesville, USA. Yet, now that I'm accustomed to the lifestyle, I'll probably live longer. If I'm stuck waiting behind a 90 year old in a gigantic 1968 Cadillac Sedan de Ville, I figure I'm just where I should be. If I sped up and made that light, perhaps I'd be t-boned at the intersection. What can I do if the propeller doesn't function properly on the sightseeing aircraft I'm supposed to be astonished on? I'll tell you what; I'm going to wait happily and thank baby Jesus I wasn't on that sucker when it spiraled to the ground.

On rare occasions you may have heard someone utter that a person has the "patience of a saint" or that "Patience is a virtue."

Patience is also a powerful psychological medicine. Imagine what a daily mega dose of it would accomplish: Fewer incidents of ulcers, heart problems, road rage, facial wrinkles, and childish behavior from children and adults. Whether you "count to ten," take a chill pill (literally or figuratively; hopefully the latter), or become canonized and don't have to worry about waiting patiently any more, let's try to exhibit a little more self-control every day when we're waiting, and waiting, and waiting . . .

Satisfaction

PERHAPS THE FIRST SATISFYING thing that comes to mind is Mick Jagger writhing and singing the Stones' iconic tune. Naturally, sexual satisfaction comes in at a close second depending on your proclivities. (Now, that topic is out of the way.) Satisfaction means you are feeling pleased with the outcome of something.

I feel exceptionally satisfied after I put a liplock on a dee-lish dessert, meal, or piece of confectionery. Unless you are a lifelong serial killer, a child's smile or spontaneous laugh can be one of the most satisfying events of your day. Talk to me about sunsets with a glass of liquid butta, my nickname for Santa Margherita Pino Grigio.

Isn't it perfectly satisfying when you actually pass a test you studied your brains out for and were terrified you'd fail? When I took my first computerized state examination I was completely freaked out by the format and intensely confusing wording of each question and multiple choice answer. Just in case I bombed, I actually concocted lies to tell my associates so they wouldn't discover my lack of success.

Satisfaction can mean losing a lousy pound in a week or finally shedding those last few ounces of blubber. I know I'm totally satisfied when I can slip into a dress that's a size smaller. Satisfaction can be as uncomplicated as completing a sand castle and the waves not erasing your architectural delight in front of your sensitive eyes. How about when a baby finally stops crying or when a puppy ceases to yelp when you need some long lost shut-eye? That's the most super characteristic of satisfaction; it can come in a million forms.

Oh, Lord, I just tremble with satisfaction when my eyes open on the first morning of a vacation even if I am in my own bed in a hurricane and not at some fancy-schmancy spa resort in Bali. (Please take me with you when you go.) How about that overwhelming sensation of satisfaction when you write the LAST check for your mortgage, car, or credit card? Paying off a debt is mucho satisfying. On the other hand after the guilt subsides, the sense of satisfaction is breathtaking when you purchase something that is totally frivolous like a useless matching pitcher, creamer, and sugar bowl which will eventually join the others in the back of your kitchen cabinet. I know you are thinking of that 99th pair of shoes or that driver that guarantees a hole in one not to mention that wrinkle eraser which you know won't work and the cure-all arthritis bracelet that gives you a rash.

An initial sense of satisfaction can be coupled with laughter, regret, depression, bankruptcy, or a mother of a migraine if you don't reign yourself in sometimes. But, who cares? What harm can a little bit of immediate satisfaction do? Let me count the ways . . .

Promises

A PROMISE IS A THOUGHT which is often spoken in a breath. Even if a promise is written, it can be fragile. Given time and the right set of circumstances, promises can solidify in a sense which can be beneficial or not.

Time passes quickly unless you are unhappy. Seven years can seem like seventy-seven. "I promise I'll love you forever and ever," she seductively whispered during their wedding ceremony. Fortunately, they both decided that their union was of a temporary nature seven years later. Is that an acute attack of the seven-year itch, or what? On the other hand, my parents were married for fifty-four years and didn't want to be far from one another for very long. They kept as many promises as they could.

Blood brothers make a declaration of loyalty to one another. A blood oath can be a symbol of unity between individuals and tribes, or among troops. I've read that you'd better think twice when you pinky swear in Japan where the practice began. Today, we refer to a pinky swear as a casual way of sealing a promise. I wouldn't suggest making a pinky swear in Japan around 1640. Heaven help you if you lied. Your little finger would have been amputated. You'd get punched with a fist something like ten-thousand times, and, my favorite of all, you'd have to swallow thousands of needles. Think I'll hang out by myself and not make any promises ever.

Sometimes you know you are going to break your promise while you are making it. You may do that to save someone's feelings or to preserve your sanity. Personally, I try to stay clear of taking oaths. Life is like water; always changing its course. A humongous promise could cause the likes of an embolism in a relationship.

Promises can lift spirits but rip households apart. A leader promises to protect a homeland. The population cheers. Soldiers vow to protect their country. It becomes a catch-22 because one or more individuals leave home in order to safeguard a beloved family. Too many people around the world are trapped within this paradox. History keeps repeating itself but we never learn.

Many promises are made too lightly these days. "No problem with the telephone and electricity bills. Your child support check is on its way." People's well-beings are at stake. Promises of this sort must be kept.

Some promises are just plain stupid and unattainable which make you feel like a failure. "I promise to just drink water, eat only protein, and not one carb will enter my mouth for the next twelve months. Oh, yeah, I'll go to the gym every morning for an hour before work and on Saturdays." Hello, typical New Year's Eve promise broken by an infinite number of people in The Land of Chubsters a.k.a. the USA.

A pact is a mother of a promise because liability under international law is at stake. It has been said that the recent climate change pact in Paris is beneficial to humans because of proposed pollution control measures. In turn, fewer damaging storms would result in less of a drain on the global economy. Hey, I'm for cleaner air and not taxing the economy. I want the biggest Social Security check possible when the time comes. (I hear smug laughter in the background as "they" say there will be no more Social Security payments made to retirees in the relatively near future. Loud GULPS are heard from fearful Americans.)

A treaty is the grandmamma of all promises because it is an international pinky swear. Felicitations to my dear old social studies classes when we learned about the Treaty of Versailles which officially ended World War I in 1919. Now, THAT was a big time promise.

Informed promises are the most important ones. Let's pledge that if we agree to participate in a contract of any sort that we will enter into it with as much knowledge as possible, a clear conscience, and an open heart. Then, you won't have to hear "you broke your promise" which sounds pitiful in any language.

Weather

WEATHER CAN DEFINITELY affect your temperament, health, and sense of general well-being. A magnificent dusk can take your breath away as you sit with a cold beverage, feet up, ignoring the ghastly news on the tube, and mutter to yourself, "Ah, my day wasn't that bad. There's always tomorrow."

I grew up thirty minutes north of Manhattan. I clearly remember four distinct seasons until I was about twenty. An imperceptible change occurred after that time. Inexplicable pink tinted clouds appeared when there was neither a sunrise nor a sunset.

Winter was cold, snowy, and lots of fun. Who didn't enjoy having the wits scared out of them on a wild toboggan ride or crashing your sled? Remember Flying Saucers; how deadly were they? I never saw one that was not seriously dented. How revitalizing to see crocuses peek through the thawing ground. Sorry, peops, spring lasted for about ten minutes even back then. That was still long enough to make millions of eyes red and itchy. Noses dripped because of thick blankets of pollen. You could actually draw pictures in that green powder. We had luscious wisteria vines on our property. The bumblebees were so big that they had landing gear.

All too soon we were blasted straight into the furnace of an overly long summer. Remember baking in the sun all slathered up in oil so you'd fry faster? Lifeguards were the only ones who used sunblock. They used schmears of thick white zinc oxide cream on their noses and only if it reached the second degree burn stage.

The changing colors of fall leaves were a pleasure but snow often appeared when it was least expected. One image that sticks in my mind is of crimson leaves uncharacteristically covered with pristine flakes. It was a gorgeous sight but rather disturbing in a "Has Mother Nature completely lost her mind?" kind of way. The seasonal cycle continued to become more distorted with each passing year but climate change doesn't exist; right? Try asking a polar bear.

As I matured and moved to Boston I began to understand why the weather was being altered. I could smell the pollution of New Jersey miles before I passed though it on my way home to New York. I eventually moved to Manhattan and found disarming amounts of soot on my window sills and face. What freaked me out was that I was inhaling that black poison every day. I felt like an urban Coal Miner's Daughter.

A boisterous thunderstorm or a few snow days off from school were about as intense as the weather got when I was growing up. Now, I live in Florida. Hurricane season lasts from June through December and can make you jittery even in you live up North. To make matters worse, tornado alerts and warnings seem to be the newest fad. These days a tropical wave can travel, intensify, transform into a hurricane, and create billions of dollars of damage in the northeast. Who thought Manhattan's subways could be flooded and shut down due to "Superstorm Sandy?"

I cried like a toddler during my first hurricane in October, 2006. Hilda was a real doozy. My dad snoozed while I clutched our poodle and watched pieces of trailers fly down the street, trees snap in half, and 50-year-old shrubbery with deep roots scatter like tumbleweeds. It was still hot and no electricity meant no air conditioning. You were out of luck unless you had a generator and gas stove. People barbecued and used Sterno to cook meals and heat liquids. Families had to eat as much as they could before everything in their refrigerators and freezers putrefied. Police rushed into grocery stores to stop the pillaging of spoiled goods. Streetlights didn't work. It was pure madness that never seemed to reach the national news. The chaos continued for weeks. Fortunately, our home was on the same grid as a major hospital so we got our power back in three days. In the poorer sections of town and to the north of us, my students reported that they didn't have electricity after more than a month.

Not setting up camp or building a home along the San Andreas Fault or at the base of a mountain famous for its avalanches seem like sensible decisions. I could never comprehend why people would live along the Mississippi River. Who in their right mind would reside in a place nicknamed Tornado Alley? Would I relocate to where active volcanoes bubble up beside me such as in Hawaii or anything remotely close to the infamous Ring of Fire? Would I live in the land of typhoons? Take a guess.

I had to relocate to Florida from New York City to care for my ailing parents. I actually adore the subtropical climate. I'm told your blood thins after a while because you don't have to keep yourself warm like a Yeti anymore. I run for a sweater if it hits the eighty degree mark.

Florida is the lightning capital of the United States; how proud am I? Not. Telephone, television, and computer services are interrupted frequently during hurricane season. Granted, it's inconvenient but not life-threatening. I prepare as well as I can for a hurricane and keep extras of everything around just in case. I figure if I die in a storm, I won't have to pay any more bills.

As I age I understand that in many cases people are often drawn to the place where they were born and raised, be it heaven or hell. If you relocate, you can be lucky enough to get used to the place. You might even morph into a loyal resident like me.

Kids

ONE OF MY ELEMENTARY school teachers loudly proclaimed that it was an insult to call children kids, "Kids are baby goats!" We were horrified. Naturally, I was a kid once, a pretty wild, rotten, morose (if I was at home), tomboy sort of kid. I adored the TV show, The Rifleman, with Chuck Connors. As a Christmas gift I received a toy Winchester rifle that I prized because it looked like the real deal. It was a heavy brown beast which was able to "shoot." When I pressed the trigger exploding caps provided a semi-realistic explosion that was accompanied by the stinking smell of burning sulfur. What a charming gift for an impressionable kid.

I was an only child but never lonely. I'm a Gemini so if I were abandoned on a deserted island, I could keep myself amused for decades. On my block there were eleven kids to play with ranging in age from five to thirteen. Some were musically, comedically, or academically inclined. Others were soldiers from birth or as passive as goldfish. Everyone adored my tree house. We had a blast for years. After a few drinkies, even my folks and their friends climbed up and made themselves at home. You could hear the squeals and laughter well into the night. It was incredibly amusing to peek through my bedroom blinds and see adults acting just like kids.

Familial traditions unify individuals and are appreciated by kids. Going to Playland Amusement Park in Rye, New York was a birthday ritual that I relished. My parents and I sped up the Hutchinson River

Parkway because we treasured my day-long celebration by the shore. Sometimes even the best laid plans can go awry.

This captivating outdoor recreational area has been a favorite family stomping ground since 1928. The unnerving "Dragon Coaster" still serves as its mascot and is one of approximately one hundred wooden roller coasters still operating in the United States. I was very disappointed that I was too short to ride this famous monster. Dad decided that an appropriate alternative would be to hop aboard "The Wild Mouse." We were the only people in line for this excursion into hades. That should have been a hint right there.

My father and I innocently lowered ourselves into a metal rodent. Much to our dismay we travelled faster than the speed of light on rickety tracks that were stacked sky high. I sat in the front of our solitary car between my father's legs. We careened around sharp curves which gave us the impression that we were going to die every few seconds. I panicked and ripped handfuls of hair from my dad's lower limbs which were plastered around my frame. The pain was so excruciating that he wailed like a banshee. A crowd gathered below "The Wild Mouse" as we hurtled through the air. My father turned out to be the biggest attraction at Playland that day.

Kids simply want to be loved. They need guidance at home and at school. Freedom to pursue their interests and play are natural born rights. Kids deserve respect because they are the citizens of tomorrow.

Every day kids from kindergarten through fifth grade give me a spontaneous hug. They aren't getting cuddled enough at home. Even though it used to drive me crazy, my mother embraced me and said that she loved me even when I was asleep. Ma wanted to be sure that if anything happened, I would be positive of her feelings towards me. Funny thing is, many years later, I do the same darn thing. Every time I leave the house or go off to Slumberland I say, "I love you." Ya never know.

Spark

DIFFERENT IDEAS come to mind when you hear any derivation of the word spark. I immediately imagine a chipper wiry pup named Sparky dashing across the yard hoping for a biscuit and some roughhousing. If you are mechanically inclined perhaps spark plugs were the words you considered. Who knew how much we would depend on those babies? The unscrewing and disposing of a spark plug is the perfect revenge crime and no one gets hurt. A history buff might have thoughts of sparks from a flint which started fires for cave people. A couch potato may recollect stories of modern day sparks flying, literally and figuratively, on reality shows like Survivor and, God help us all, Naked and Afraid. Where the heck do they find these people anyway? "Sure, I'll get baked and bitten where the sun doesn't shine for a chance at a few bucks, fifteen minutes of fame, and a lifelong battle with intestinal parasites. Count me in."

We've all hoped for that spark of genius in a child's eyes or praise the heavens, in a mirror. All teachers pray for a single spark of interest in one of our students' brains at any time of the day or night. A spark in a kid's dream can turn into a raging research project and then we're all home free for a while.

Remember when your six-year-old brain tricked you into believing that anything that sparkled made it look better? Admit it; you mistakenly thought your very first school posters and book report covers were divine with a few ounces of glitter on them. Content isn't everything especially when you wrote the same nonsensical sentence in a dozen different ways. Once I discovered reflecting particles there was no stopping me: Sparkling eye shadow, hair spray, body highlights, clothing, and shoes. How did entertainers ever succeed without sparkling white porcelain veneers?

I purchased a Chevy Cruze but not before Auto Nation tried to shove a Chevrolet Spark down my throat. I'd never heard of the vehicle. Supposedly it's a relatively inexpensive "competitor with the MINI-Cooper and Fiat 500, and a fuel-efficient car that turns heads." Not mine.

Since I hardly ever use my prehistoric flip cell phone, I refuse to purchase the gazillionth app named Spark. This brilliant invention will supposedly assist me when my email inbox becomes overwhelmed; *pulllease*. I'm overwhelmed thinking of yet another app.

Ever felt butterflies in your stomach or had a certain somebody creep into your dreams? Well, that's the ever-popular and longed-for electrical spark of love or lust. It doesn't matter which one; both are delightful. No matter what your age, be it eight or eighty-eight, that spark in your heart and gut lets you know that you are alive and kickin'. Here's to your next spark.

Birthdays

I ADORE BIRTHDAYS. It's a guaranteed swell day that we get sole credit for even though our mothers still shudder from the thought of long ago contractions, labor, stretch marks, and those ten pounds that won't ever go away. The way I figure it, even if you die on your birthday, that's a gift too. Think of it: No more work, wrinkles, presidential elections, nagging, taxes, and bills. Don't worry; no one lives forever. You'll eventually get to see your friends and loved ones at those pearly gates.

Delusional behavior overcomes me before my birthday. I purchase a big ticket item like a leather couch, a walk-in bathtub, or a new head. Sprucing things up around the house and in my closet is also a must. My 20-year-old refrigerator finally dies. It's only practical for me to also buy a new stove, dishwasher, and microwave. Why? It's my birthday month. Don't kid yourself. I'm a Special Ed teacher so I charge everything and convince myself and my accountant that it's all an investment. Except for my actual birthday...

This year I dutifully visited the gym after work only to hear, "What are you doing here? It's your birthday. Go do something fun." It was the perfect time to cash in on my lifelong membership for a free serving at The Ice Cream Club. After I flashed my driver's license and entered into a state of frozen bliss, I pondered on what I really wanted to do. It was an absolutely perfect afternoon in May in South Florida.

Sure, I could take advantage of gift certificates that I'd been given but I thought, "Been there; done that. I'll use them over my summer break." Then, it came to me. What I imagined was a helicopter ride along the coastline with a hunk of burnin' love. Within an hour I was soaring above Donald Trump's Mar-a-Lago Club on my left and gaping at manta rays and sharks on my right. I was airborne with my pilot, handsome Mark, in a giant metal mosquito.

Before our flight it was explained to me that our 'copter weighed approximately 850 pounds fully fueled. To my amazement Mark was actually able to pull it by the tail boom and hook it up to a golf cart. We taxied down the tarmac hauling my dream come true. As I examined my birthday treat I realized that there were no doors, only twelve extra inches beyond my toes in the nose of the mini- helicopter, and not enough room for a hair between us in the cockpit. As we rose into the air I gestured how wonderful everything looked. My left arm snapped back in the wind. (No doors; remember?) I quickly secured my hand against my chest as Mark chuckled and suggested that I experiment with aerodynamics with my forearm in the wind. I politely declined.

The next morning I was still tripping with joy and excitement. I told some people about my fabulous adventure. More than a few told me of their buried birthday wishes. I tried to convince them that we all deserve extra smiles in our lives even if the checkbook or VISA runs screaming at our approach. All I'm sure of is that there is a new birthday tradition at my house and it involves rotor blades.

Vacations

WHEN DID THE VAST majority of the population stop caring about how they look when they travel? Almost everyone at the airport appears to have rolled out of bed, dressed in total darkness in someone else's clothes, and been dumped on the sidewalk at a random airline. Their luggage resembles remnants from a war zone. Why don't folks print out their boarding passes instead of standing in endless lines liked drugged penguins? Please explain the reason behind travelling with children whose age bracket falls within the terrible twos range. (Let grandma visit you for God's sake.) How do individuals surpassing an average weight and height fit into the cramped seats of the flying sardine cans known as modern jets? There is always the lingering fear of a terrorist attack on one of the legs of a trip. So, why pray tell, do we go on holidays at all?

Everyone deserves a vacation. Even if you are jobless, you still deserve time off from seeking employment. Creating a résumé, being interrogated on interviews, and selling yourself are incredibly stressful pursuits. The anxiety of not paying bills on time, the hope of making a decent salary, and prayers for medical benefits are fuel for more headaches and wrinkles. Searching for a position that doesn't suck the brain out of your skull and actually allows you to eat meals other than oatmeal, beans, and week-old bread can cause depression, a lack of self-esteem, and, in turn, a sincere desire to get away from it all.

Many people have more than one job. That's double the reason to want to hop a plane to any-freakin'-where. I'm a Special Ed teacher and often tutor or teach summer school to earn extra bucks. I couldn't even remember when or where my last vacation was. That's when I decided to give a big heave-ho to all responsibilities and burn a hole in my pocketbook. Upon my departure I told my neighbors NOT to call me if my dog dies or my home burns down. You only live once; right? (I certainly hope so but that's another story.)

Personally, a dream destination is somewhere I've never been and off the beaten track. How about a bicycle tour, riding horses, climbing through lava tubes, hiking to waterfalls and geysers, fishing, swimming in geo-thermal lagoons, eating flavorsome foods, drinking a mysterious booze nicknamed The Black Death, and sightseeing from a comfortable coach with my derrière planted in a cozy seat after all of my activities? You got a deal. Book my flight to Iceland, pronto.

First of all, Iceland should have been named Greenland and vice versa. Icelandic rain can be horizontal, cutting winds come from all directions, and there is a prolonged time of darkness from mid-November to the end of January. However, during the summer months temperatures can be in the 50's and low 60's during the day. Hint: Wear layers of clothing. No reason to be scared if you travel alone; there's no nighttime. There are special curtains so you can get your beauty sleep in a blackened room.

This northern European country is so clean you can serve a meal in every public bathroom. The air is crisp and clean. There is no garbage anywhere. I saw three cops in two weeks and they were laughing with each other. This haven has no army, navy, or air force. It's been voted the most peaceful nation for ten years in a row. If there's an important soccer game, huge outdoor screens are set up in convenient areas so the community can share its excitement and national pride. Everyone speaks English. You don't even have to exchange any money because credit cards are accepted for the smallest purchases. Best news ever: Iceland is less than a six hour flight from New York. Are you ready to fly the coop?

The worst part of any vacation is U. S. Customs. It took fifteen minutes to walk from my plane only to join untold masses of humanity in a line to have a chat with an agent. After picking up my luggage, I had to drag it to a re-check point, search for a bus, and wait for another plane. Thank heavens my overlay was three hours long because it took two hours to get to my connecting flight's gate. By that time, I was more exhausted and hungry than after my subterranean volcano explorations.

Just give me another year or so to save my pennies and try to erase the memories of going through customs. I'll be ready for another well-deserved vacation. In the meantime, I'll be fantasizing about faraway lands like Japan, Australia, and New Zealand. Have I got you thinking about a vay-kay?

Coffee

I REALLY DISLIKE almost everything about coffee. Think of the stain it leaves on your teeth and clothing. Oh, the joy of coffee breath which unfortunately can be upstaged by the infamous combination of coffee/cigarette breath. That's a deal breaker for sure. What about the jitters and headaches from an overdose of caffeine? Those are charming, especially for loved ones and co-workers. I'll have to give a pass to coffee ice cream and that delectable Italian dessert, Tiramisu, which literally means "a pick me up." It should be translated as "makes you incredibly fat" because there must be 10,000 calories in each serving.

The so-called aroma of coffee makes me run for the hills and I don't mean Juan Valdez's Colombian mountaintops. In Barnes & Noble I can at least escape to the music section on the other side of the store while my friends stand in line for expensive sludge. I'm out of luck in those cozy cafes where I sit and pray for an oxygen mask. How about being trapped in a car while my passengers linger over their God awful Dunkin' Donuts brew? (They can't even spell "doughnut" correctly but that's another pet peeve.)

Can you think of anyone addicted enough to have Starbucks *deliver* a cup o' Joe when the fee is more than the coffee? You have to tip; remember? That's one way to put a burning hole in your pocket. Let's put it this way: I'd rather visit Java with its bubbling volcanoes than guzzle a steaming mug of java. You'll find me doing lots of things but craving a cup of muddy water isn't one of them.

Advice

ADVICE HAS BEEN AROUND for as long as living things have existed. Even animals advise each other with their actions and sounds. Ever see a lioness pick up her cub by the back of the neck? You can envision her thinking, "You little dope, you are going to get eaten if you don't stay put!"

I'd venture to say that advice is generally given with the hope that it will help matters even if you want to slug the advisor in a Donald Trump type of way. There are innumerable ways to give advice. You can flat out declare your romantic recommendations free-of-charge, "You really shouldn't date your own brother." Or, you can send an anonymous letter even though texting is a favored method these days. It's the sign of the times to announce the unpleasantries of your personal life and post them along with incriminating photographs on Facebook. You're sure to receive guidance on how to revamp your paltry life from people you don't even know.

I cringe when I hear financial advice. It's just a crap shoot any way you look at it. I watched a news report that aired the results of a yearlong competition between one of New Jersey's topnotch stockbrokers and a chimpanzee. The ape spun the guy's Rolodex and randomly chose securities to invest in while the adviser crunched his magic numbers. They both spent the same amount of money on each transaction. After twelve months of wheeling and dealing, the chimp won. (The sound of money being shoved under mattresses is heard.)

My suggestion would be to stay away from the advice of zealots and intoxicated people. There's a big difference between a sounding board and an old-fashioned brainwashing. A guidance counsellor, family member, friend, psychiatrist, or a concerned mentor is quite different from the likes of a well-oiled delusional stranger, Svengali, or a Jim Jones Kool-Aid drinking cult leader.

A popular piece of advice is often given by professionals, "Never sleep with anyone at work." I've heard it said using more colorful language. Just picture the boss's spouse screaming over another affair with an assistant.

There's advice on how to live your life and what politics to believe in spouted from the mouths of Buddha, Stalin, Ghandi, all the way to your next door neighbor's opinion. There's also generic advice that you hear at graduations like "Live up to your potential!" which is easier said than done.

On occasion individuals believe that the best advice is to do nothing. I've read that some natives of New Guinea actually allow their young ones to get burned if they get too close to a fire because the kids never make that mistake twice. I know that I didn't touch the top of the double-broiler on our old stove more than once. No seconds on advice needed there.

Erica Jong's opinion about decision-making rings true. In How to Save Your Own Life, she wrote, "Advice is what we ask for when we already know the answer but wish we didn't." If you're still not sure after consulting yourself and some pals, reading is an excellent way to get advice on virtually any topic. Simply go to the library or your computer's friendly nonjudgmental search engine. Take helpful information from someone who has experience and disregard the rest.

I'm the Queen of Self-Help books. In order to ward off premature drooling, memory loss, and staring into space, an artistic colleague advised me of the benefits of drawing with my sub-dominant hand. That was challenging advice for my brain and I'm still coherent. Ancient Chinese philosophy certainly takes the edge off everyday problems. The Sermon on the Mount contains many words of wise advice, "…seek, and you will find; …"

Last but not least, there's self-serving advice such as if I were to suggest that you reread this book. I do think it's worth considering; don't you?

About the Author

C LAUDINE SEIBERT earned a master's degree in education from Columbia University. She then became a Montessori teacher in Manhattan and Connecticut and now thrives as a special education teacher in Florida. She savors time composing satirical vignettes with just the perfect sprinkling of practical guidance.

For more information, please go to **www.claudineseibert.com**.